"LET US RISE UP AND BUILD..." (Neh. 2:18b)

THE CHURCH —

WITHIN (Col. 1:27)
&
WITHOUT! (Matt. 16:18)

By:
Charles R. Solomon, Ed.D.
Author of *Handbook to Happiness*

"LET US RISE UP AND BUILD..." the Church!

© 2011 by Charles R. Solomon
All rights reserved. No part of this book may be reproduced or transmitted in any form or by any means without written permission of the author.

Published by
Solomon Publications
P. O. Box 6115
Sevierville, TN 37864   USA

GraceFellowshipIntl.com
SolomonPublications.org
Phone: (865) 429-0450
chuckgfi@aol.com

ISBN 978-0-9819865-8-6

Printed by
Lightning Source Inc.
www.lightningsource.com

Cover Design by
Mark Phillips
mark@marksphillips.com

Scripture quotations (unless indicated otherwise)
are from The Holy Bible, King James Version

"LET US RISE UP AND BUILD..." the Church— Within & Without!

TABLE OF CONTENTS

Chapter	Title	Page
	Introduction	7
PART 1	**The Church Within**	**17**
1	Burden and Call	19
2	Surveying the Broken Walls	25
3	Repairing the Walls	39
4	Sanballat and Tobiah!	55
5	Joining Hands with Others—Past and Present	61
6	A New Reformation	69
7	The Praise of Ezra and Ours!	77

TABLE OF CONTENTS

PART II	**The Church Without**	81
	An Overview	83
	Epilogue	99
	Resources	115

INTRODUCTION

Since the Reformation, and particularly in recent decades, the foundation of justification has been meticulously laid. In fact, it continues to be laid again and again, while the superstructure of discipleship or sanctification usually goes begging.

The well honed arguments for the various aspects of justification make good theological fodder, but are of little avail in building the Christian life on the only Foundation, the Lord Jesus Christ (1 Cor. 3:11). Since the reformers were vitally concerned with laying the foundation of justification by faith, they had little time, or inclination, to build discipleship or sanctification—the superstructure—on the sure foundation.

In the five centuries which have transpired since then, the fallout from that pivotal era has continued to consist of a greater emphasis on justification, or receiving new life, with that which is built on that foundation being frequently attempted by self-effort (Gal. 3:3).

While I firmly endorse building a solid foundation and continuing to do so for unbelievers, a foundation without a superstructure is of little use in fulfilling the Great Commission.

The superstructure of discipleship or sanctification derives its blueprint from the preaching of the cross (1 Cor. 1:18). The lack of such, as a major emphasis, has resulted in a Church that is lacking in power. We are admonished in Hebrews 6:1:

> *Therefore leaving the principles of the doctrine of Christ, let us go on unto perfection (maturity); not laying again the foundation of repentance from dead works, and of faith toward God.*

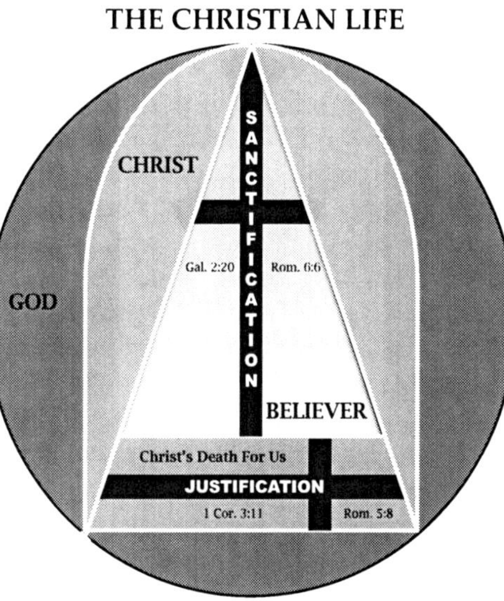
THE CHRISTIAN LIFE
CHRIST
SANCTIFICATION
Gal. 2:20
Rom. 6:6
GOD
BELIEVER
Christ's Death For Us
JUSTIFICATION
1 Cor. 3:11
Rom. 5:8

I am in my Father, and ye in Me, and I in you. John 14:20

Christ in you, the hope of Glory. Col. 1:27

The above model of the Christian life depicts sanctification as the superstructure or 'walls' to which I am referring here. Since we, as believers, are the Church, the superstructure is being built within us so we are always under construction. (You may read a more complete account of this model in my book, *The Romans Road: From the Wilderness to Canaan*.) Through the centuries since the Reformation, there has continually been greater emphasis on justification, with dynamic sanctification being overlooked. The cross in justification has been dutifully preached, but the cross in sanctification has received much less emphasis.

'Building the walls of the Church', rather than continuing the numerical church growth focus, will result in maturing believers and transformed lives, as we have found at GFI for the last four decades. Scriptural discipleship begins with the experienced cross (Luke 14:27, Gal. 2:20, Rom. 6:6) or the continual filling of the Spirit (Eph. 5:18). This seems to be the same 'stuff' of which true revival is made!

'Rebuilding the walls' to first century specifications demands equal emphasis on sanctification or discipleship that has been

Introduction

accorded justification. Since the seven last words of the Church are: "We haven't done it this way before", we will no doubt encounter some Sanballats and Tobiahs as the rebuilding effort is begun (Neh. 2:10)!

This book will also counter some of the common objections that critics have hurled through the years at Christ-centered counseling. The most common objection has been, "It is too simplistic". However, God has been faithful to transform lives, despite the lack of recognition from mainstream Christian counseling.

If I had waited for the organized Church to promote a spiritual approach to discipleship counseling, I would yet be waiting! However, God has been faithful to His calling in 1967; and lives have been transformed to His glory on six continents.

My foundational book, *Handbook to Happiness* (Tyndale), has now been in print (and more recently, ebook) since January 1972 and has been a resource, if not inspiration, for many other ministries.

"Let Us Rise Up and Build..." the Church!

I invite you to join what God is, and has been, doing: *Come, and let us build!* (Neh. 2:17b), while there is yet a window of opportunity.

Introduction

SANCTIFICATION SIMPLIFIED

Sanctification is a subject
Where definition is evasive;
When clouded with theology,
Meanings can be persuasive.
As with most important things,
Keeping it simple is good;
This will result in the rank and file's
Knowing it is understood.

Justification is receiving life,
While sanctification is living it;
Neither is the product of self-effort,
With the Holy Spirit's giving it.
When we are convicted of our sin,
We're candidates for justification;
Being convicted of our flesh,
We are prepared for sanctification.

Justification by faith was the cry,
When the Reformation was going strong;
But equal emphasis on holy living
To the Reformation did not belong.

"Let Us Rise Up and Build..." the Church!

Absent the centrality of the Cross,
Today's Church is lacking power;
Only as it returns to preaching the cross, (1 Cor. 1:18)
Will it cease to retreat and cower.

We must lose our life at the cross (Luke 9:23,24)
If we are to know resurrection;
But educating the flesh to perform (Gal.3:3)
Has substituted for co-crucifixion.
While losing our lives is unpopular,
It is the only way of the Cross;
Not losing our lives, but saving them,
We will surely suffer loss.

Only a new Reformation will suffice,
Where the cry is sanctification by faith;
Only then will we realize
The power that raised Jesus from death. (Eph. 1:18,19)
Ours must be a life out of death, (Gal. 2:20, Rom. 6:6)
If it is to be resurrection life—
With sanctification a life, not a theory,
The Spirit's giving peace for our strife.

The time for spinning theories
Must be replaced with lives transformed;
Which can only be our lot
As to Jesus' life we're conformed. (Rom. 8:29)

Introduction

Educating the flesh will be out of vogue
When true discipleship is done; (Luke 14:27)
Only then will we know Christ as Life
And victory when the race is run.

C. R. Solomon
April 16, 2010

"Let Us Rise Up and Build…" the Church!

PART I

THE CHURCH WITHIN
(Col. 1:27)

"Let Us Rise Up and Build..." the Church!

CHAPTER 1

BURDEN & CALL

Nehemiah received word that the walls of Jerusalem were broken down, and this news caused him much grief. Similarly, I was to experience the deficiency of the Church first hand. My intense spiritual need drove me to seek answers which I was not to find in the Church.

Though I identified with a conservative local body of believers and became active in its ministry, it offered little beyond the basics of salvation. Having been steeped in the truth of justification without resolution of long standing spiritual and psychological issues, I was left to the Holy Spirit and the Bible to search for the answer to my dilemma.

After years of searching, the Holy Spirit illuminated Galatians 2:20 (which I had memorized several years before) and transformed my life in a crisis experience in 1965. However, my church could not ground me in this truth so I floundered in self-study of the Word and devotional literature for the next two years. Eventually, the Spirit let me know that He could deliver others just as He had me, and called me to such a ministry. This was confirmed by Isaiah 58:10,11.

> *And if thou draw out thy soul to the hungry, and satisfy the afflicted soul; then shall thy light rise in obscurity, and thy darkness be as the noon day: And the LORD shall guide thee continually, and satisfy thy soul in drought, and make fat thy bones: and thou shalt be like a watered garden, and like a spring of water, whose waters fail not.*

Burden and Call

Since I was neither led *to* nor *in* this new quality of life in the body of believers, it follows that I was not encouraged in my preparation for ministry in my late 30's, except by two brothers who became my first board members.

Though I made every effort to relate to my local church, my quest for spiritual growth and education for the ministry was *despite* the Church, rather than *because* of it.

Thus, I learned firsthand that the walls of the Church—the superstructure of sanctification—were in gross need of repair. This book chronicles how the beginnings of repair have taken place over the past 40 years. My burden is for widespread continuation of this rebuilding, that hurting believers can find *cure* inside the Church, as contrasted with *care* outside of it.

I invite you to join us in the preparation of the Church for ministry to the saved as well as the lost!

"Let Us Rise Up and Build..." the Church!

NOTE: My testimony, in some detail, is recounted in Part II of my second book, *The Ins and Out of Rejection*.

Burden and Call

THE CALL OF GOD
Isaiah 58:10-14

God's calling on my life
Was to *satisfy the afflicted soul*; (v. 10)
Through knowing Christ as Life,
They could be made whole.
He promised to guide my way
That obscurity not prevail, (v. 10b)
And to satisfy my soul
As dryness He did reveal.

I would *be like a watered garden* (v. 11b)
And like a spring unfailing,
That those who follow after (v. 12a)
Would see their work prevailing.
They will build up barren venues—
Foundations of many generations; (v. 12b)
They will repair the void,
Which is common to all nations.

My purpose is to honor Him—
Not doing my own ways,
Nor finding my own pleasure, (v. 13b)
Speaking His words all my days.

"Let Us Rise Up and Build..." the Church!

Then I can delight myself in Him (v. 14a)
And travel on earth's *high places*;
As with Jacob, so with me, (v. 14b)
The Word from His mouth He graces.

CHAPTER 2

SURVEYING THE BROKEN WALLS
(Neh. 2:13)

Nehemiah went to Jerusalem and saw for himself the exact state of the walls. Similarly, I would like to view the deficiencies which are rampant in today's Church under the following headings:

1. Lack of spiritual maturity on the part of pastor and people

    As I have counseled and talked with pastors over the years, I find that most who come to the cross in experience have been in the ministry for several, to many, years before they come to this understanding or illumination. Recently, we had a pastor come into victory after having pastored the same Baptist church for 34 years. Another was retired at 69 when the cross became a reality, after having been saved at 21.

Obviously, such pastors could not lead their congregation where they had not been! The great missionary to China, Hudson Taylor, needed to have the breakthrough, also. He had been on the mission field 10-15 years before his life was changed (exchanged!), resulting in his excellent biography, *Hudson Taylor's Spiritual Secret*. Also, V. Raymond Edmond documented 20 such testimonies in his fine book, *They Found the Secret*. My recent book, *Pastors to Pastors, Testimonies of Revitalized Ministries* is also written in this vein.

2. An inadequate understanding of discipleship may be responsible for few coming to personal knowledge of identification with Christ. In many quarters, a disciple is merely a 'learner' and does

not have to *lose his life* to do so, despite the admonition of Luke 14:27:

> *And whosoever doth not bear his cross, and come after me, cannot be my disciple.*

3. Biblical anthropology can also be a deterrent since the dichotomous view (man as body and soul only) has become the dominant position in this country. In my opinion, a consistent application of such theology would not support a co-crucifixion with Christ (Rom 6:6). If there is no spirit, as a separate functioning entity, there is nothing to be crucified or made new. Therefore, the general teaching emanating from this view is that of progressive sanctification that cannot be punctuated with a life-transforming breakthrough. Such a progression would be of little value in ministering to someone who is intent upon taking his life, as happens at times in discipleship counseling! I have found that the illumination

by the Spirit of the scriptural model—spirit, soul, and body (1 Thes. 5:23) has opened up the Scriptures to many.

4. Another area of weakness is that seminaries do not typically assure that the spiritual growth of the student keeps pace with his(her) theological understanding. Or, to put it another way, the students usually are not actively discipled in their home churches nor in their theological education. That being the case, he is usually left to his own devices to put the meat on the bones, so to speak. Though not all would be open to Galatians 2:20 personal mentoring, a number would be since they are purposely there for spiritual preparation for ministry. It has been estimated that fewer than 10% of believers in this country ever experience Christ as life and, probably, not more than 20% of pastors (Col. 3:1-4). I have confirmed this estimate in my reading and talking with a number of them.

5. Another criticism of Christ-centered counseling is that we are teaching sinless perfection (since they equate the crucifixion of the old man or nature with inability to sin). A main reason for this is that the flesh and old man are also equated. We believe that the old man has been put off (Col. 3:9); however, the flesh remains (Gal. 5:16,17). Sins in the believer emanate from the flesh, the world, and the devil. If it is held that all sin comes from the sin nature (*old man* of Romans 6:6) and that was literally crucified, it would follow that no sin would be possible. Therefore, it is absolutely necessary that scriptural terms be accurately defined, without overlapping.

6. The church growth movement has been a source of deficiencies in discipleship since the emphasis is frequently on 'seeker sensitive' or 'seeker friendly' approaches which tend to minimize discipleship. A leader in this movement, Willow Creek, recently published a book

which said they had many members but few disciples. If the scriptural definition of a disciple were applied, there might be even fewer! Since numbers and facilities have been equated with success, many have followed the lead of megachurches, thus increasing the shallowness of believers' lives. Thousands of churches have followed the lead of Willow Creek in an association, even though the book entitled *Reveal* by Greg Hawkins indicated that their approach was less than successful in the vital area of discipleship in the mega-church movement.

7. In tandem with the church growth movement has been the rise in popularity of Christian psychology to *care* for those for whom the Church has failed to minister *cure*! However, psychotherapy is not noted for producing disciples who have lost their lives at the cross in exchange for that of the Lord Jesus. Absent that, the flesh, or self, is strengthened as some symptoms are assuaged. One might say

that when the symptoms are alleviated the problem, the flesh, is exacerbated! However, the alleviation of symptoms (such as depression) is accepted as success since the problem, the flesh, is not usually identified as the root problem in therapy. It is my assessment that both the church growth movement and Christian psychology have peaked and are in decline. In that event, the vacuum created could well be what is needful to usher in a New Reformation—the cross for the flesh rather than therapy for the symptoms!

8. The average pastor has accepted the current thinking that counseling is a specialty limited to those with advanced education. If one is to do therapy, this is true. If we are content to allow the Holy Spirit to do His work, one with less than a high school education can be used of God to great advantage! In fact, we recently heard from a brother using my books, with the Spirit's transforming lives,

who has less than a high school education; and English is his second language. Added to that, he has had no training except telephone coaching! Since what we have been describing is, in reality, discipleship, it requires that one be a disciple, not necessarily a well educated believer.

9. Another major factor is the "*offense of the cross*" (Gal. 5:11) which is a major detriment to the faint hearted! There are those who teach the cross for the believer who opt for majoring on identity, since it is more palatable to the hearer! Though our identity in Christ is vitally important, it must be a *result*, never a *cause* of consequent behavior. Trying to live Christ's identity without having 'lost our lives' is to try and have resurrection power without crucifixion weakness! The cart is in front of the horse! Losing our lives means losing control, which is not the favorite thing of folks I have met! But if He is to take control, we must lose control. As a person comes to the end of himself

to appropriate the cross (Gal. 2:20), it always reduces to an issue of control, however defined in the individual life. As we finally allow Him to take complete control, we wonder how we could have been so dumb so long—'too soon old and too late smart'!

10. One observation that is heard frequently in church circles is that those making an emphasis on the life in Christ or the 'deeper life', are characterized by passivity. The implication is that they do little or no evangelism.

   I would like to cite one instance that counters such an allegation. Dr. Lee Turner, author of the fine study books, *Grace Disicipleship Course*, did not overtly teach on evangelism in his church, but, rather, emphasized the life in Christ and saw much evangelism take place as the overflow of those who had exchanged the self-life for the Christ-life, thereby living resurrection life.

And, at GFI, we have designed an approach to evangelism that incorporates the cross for the believer so that it is not either/or, but both/and! Tracts for use with unbelievers have been written, as well as a seminar which inculcates both Christ's death for us and our death with Him—from the beginning!

11. And, lastly, there are those who would have us make greater emphasis on confession and repentance for individual sins, which is very necessary. However, it is equally, if not more, important to deal with the source—the power or principle of indwelling sin. The first involves the Blood for sins; the second involves the Cross for the sinner (see *The Normal Christian Life* by Watchman Nee, Chapters 1 and 2), and it is our position that equal emphasis must be placed on both. With the first, the Lord Jesus died for us; with the second, we died with Him.

When we deal with the source—*sin*, we will have less of the results—*sins*—to repent and confess (Rom. 6:11). Thus, the teaching of discipleship/sanctification must parallel the teaching of justification if we are to have mature believers who not only win the lost but also disciple them in Christ.

CROSS OR NO CROSS? THAT IS THE QUESTION!

The cross in justification
Is without a serious detractor;
The cross in sanctification
Is an entirely different factor!

Some would have us believe
Sanctification is a progression—
From justification to life's end
Without need for a regression.

Coming to the end of self
And the experience of the cross, (Gal. 2:20)
Would seem to be superfluous,
If not an ultimate loss.

Some would call it two stage salvation,
For the believer to experience the cross;
But lacking dealing with the flesh,
Means the believer will suffer loss.

Surveying the Broken Walls

Until the cry, *O wretched man*, (Rom. 7:24)
The believer is in denial;
With theology buttressing the way,
It is man, not God, who's on trial.

I am crucified with Christ (Gal. 2:20)
Was declared at our justification; (Rom. 6:3-6)
The reality, ours in experience,
Is the substance of sanctification. (Luke 14:27)

Yes, there is a progression—
To the end of self's strength;
For God to make this known,
He will go to any length!

So long as self can muster
The strength to feign obedience,
The outward appearance is acceptable
As His commands we give credence.

But transformed lives are in short supply,
When on the flesh we do rely!
Having begun in the Spirit, (Gal. 3:3)
We revert to flesh as our ally!

"Let Us Rise Up and Build..." the Church!

With the cry, *O wretched man*,
The Spirit prepares us for the cross;
The progression, ever downward,
Assures that we are prevented loss.

When we are *alway delivered unto death*, (2 Cor. 4:11)
Life will result in others; (2 Cor. 4:12)
Death and resurrection with Christ (Rom. 6:3-6)
Levels the ground with our brothers.

C. R. Solomon
April 20, 2010

CHAPTER 3

REPAIRING THE WALLS (40 Years' Results — Nationally and Internationally)

In Nehemiah 2:20 we read,

> *The God of heaven, he will prosper us; therefore, we his servants will arise and build. . . .*

And build they did, with the wall being finished in fifty two days!

> *So built we the wall; and all the wall was joined together unto the half thereof; for the people had a mind to work.* (Neh. 4:6)

They used tools and their bare hands,

"Let Us Rise Up and Build..." the Church!

> *For the builders, every one had his sword girded by his side and so builded* (Neh. 4:18a).

In like manner, from the beginning, we had *the sword of the Spirit, which is the word of God* (Eph. 6:17)—not by our side but in our hands! This was augmented from the beginning in 1970 by the Line Diagram (page 42) which has been the most effective tool that God has used in the erecting of the superstructure of sanctification. Preaching or teaching the fullness of the cross from the Word must always be central, but illustrations can be the key to a believer's having illumination on this vital truth.

As our Lord used parables to drive home His teaching, so the Line Diagram could be viewed as a modern day 'parable'. Some have jokingly remarked that Jesus was drawing the Line Diagram in the sand when faced with the woman taken in adultery! (The description of the Line Diagram is also in a tract entitled *The Wheel and Line*, which has been translated in many languages.)

While the Holy Spirit is always the Therapist, this visual illustration has been used by Him to drive home the point that we were in Christ when He was crucified and raised from the dead. Therefore, it is appropriate that I repeat it here from *Handbook to Happinness* that it be at the forefront of your thinking. The Spirit has used it to illuminate the truth more than any other aid He has given us in teaching His Word.

"Let Us Rise Up and Build..." the Church!

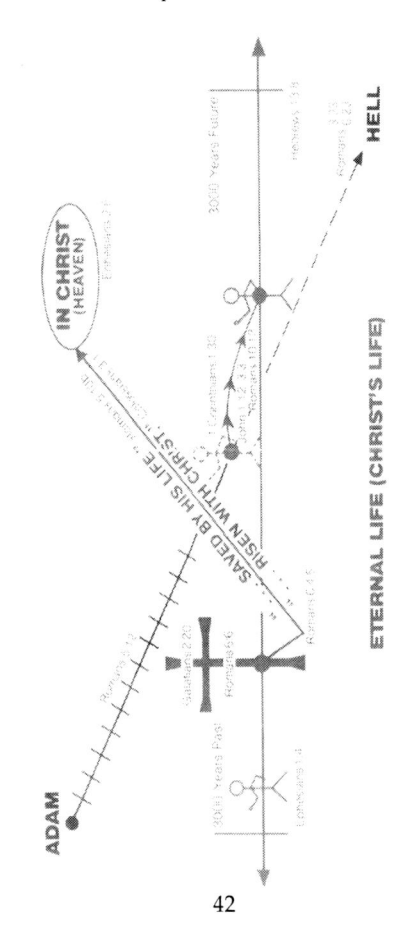

Line Diagram

The Line Diagram shows the 'life out of death' principle—God's way of disposing of internal conflict.

The horizontal line represents eternal life, the life of Christ. By definition, eternal indicates no beginning or end. It exceeds the boundaries of time. Since Christ is God, He has always lived and always will. His life is the same yesterday, today, and forever (Heb. 13:8). As portrayed at the left of the line, Christ *became flesh* (John 1:14) and lived in a human body for some 33 years. Then, He was crucified, buried, and raised from the dead on the third day (1 Cor. 15:3,4). He continues to live today (Heb. 7:25). Note that eternal life is not only a present and future reality for the believer but also involves the eternal past.

Until we are *born again* (John 3:3) we are not in the life of Christ—eternal life—but we are in the spiritually dead life or lineage of Adam. One can readily see that if any one of our ancestors, represented by the hatch marks on the diagonal line, had been missing, we also would be missing! Physically speaking, our lives had beginning in Adam. Positionally and spiritually whatever happened to him also happened to us (Rom. 5:12). When he sinned, we sinned; when he died (spiritually), we died—just as we would have died in our great-grandfather, if he had died before having any children. Thus, since spiritual death is separation from God, we were all born dead (spiritually) [Eph. 2:1]. We need forgiveness for our sins, but we also need *life*. The Lord Jesus Christ came to give us both—by dying for our sins and by giving us His resurrection life (John 10:10).

If you are a Christian, you already know this much. What you may not yet know is the following:

For the believer, physical death is the gateway from life in the world and the presence of sin, to life in Heaven and the presence of God. Similarly, another type of death is the gateway from the sinful life of Adam to the eternal life of Christ. When a person is 'born again', he in the same instant dies. He is born into the life of Christ, but he simultaneously dies out of the life of Adam

Christ comes into our lives when we believe in Him and are born again, but that is not all. We are also made *partakers* of His life—eternal life. Romans 6:3 says we are not only baptized into Jesus Christ (His life) but also into His death. We can't occupy two opposite lives at the same time—the life of Adam and the life of Christ.

Your Identity

When we receive Christ by faith, it means that His death on the cross counts as payment for our sins; but it means much more. It also means that we enter into a new life—one that extends forever into the past as well as into the future. To put it another way, we exchange our history in Adam—the bad and the good—for an eternal history in Christ; we inherit a new 'family tree'! By becoming partakers of Christ's life, we become participants in His death, burial, resurrection, ascension, and seating in the heavenlies (Rom. 6:3-6; Gal. 2:20; Eph. 2:6). He only has one life, and this is the life we receive at our new birth (1 John 5:11,12).

Unless and until we know by personal faith experience that we were crucified with Christ, we will continue to try to live *for* Christ, using the methods we learned in our old self-lives. The conflicts stemming from our history in Adam will go on plaguing and defeating us. But when, by faith, we take our rightful place at the Cross in union with Christ's death and resurrection, then—and only then—can we truly *walk in newness of life* (Rom. 6:4b) where *old things are passed away; behold, all things are become new* (2 Cor. 5:17).

The Cross experience (understanding experientially our crucifixion and resurrection with Christ) is the gateway into the Spirit-controlled life (Gal. 5:16). It is life out of death, victory out of defeat—the purpose and answer for suffering in the life of the believer. Our path to the Cross, as well as the Cross itself, is a path of suffering; but it is the only path that leads to the end of suffering.

Are you weary enough of your internal conflict and constant defeat to put an end to it by faith? *Are you willing to die to all that you are so you can live in all that He is?* To do so is to exchange the self-life for the Christ-life and be filled or controlled by the Holy Spirit. To refuse to do so is to continue a walk after the flesh and to grieve the Spirit with a continuation of conflict, suffering and defeat.

From the beginning, the Holy Spirit honored the teaching of the cross in counseling with transformed lives, many of whom would have, or had, gone to psychologists or psychiatrists. While it was, in reality, discipleship or sanctification teaching, it had to be labeled as normally understood with the term 'counseling'. Much current discipleship teaching would come under the heading of Christian disciplines.

While defeated and immature Christians found victory, most came with moderate to severe psychological difficulties which responded to a personal, Christ-centered ministry process. At the middle of last century, the Church was hostile to psychology, yet embraced it as a welcome ally two decades later! So much so, that being critical, even of Freud, could result in defensiveness (as I found with a prominent Baptist pastor)!

In the first couple of years of full time ministry, there was a pedophile set free, along with a chronic mental patient of 20 years duration who, today, would be labeled Post Traumatic Stress Disorder (PTSD). It seems that God allowed a series of such maladies to showcase His power to change lives spiritually, as contrasted with psychological and/or medical treatment. That being the case, the vast majority could have, and should have, been ministered to by the church lay people as well as the staff.

However, the Church not only embraced psychology, with the first degrees awarded by Fuller Seminary; but the Church, tacitly and then openly, has advocated psychotherapy with such lives as mentioned above. In fact, the psychology departments in seminaries regard such ailments as their turf, with pastoral counseling taking a decided back seat!

Though these early demonstrations of the Holy Spirit's power to change lives were remarkable, the church growth experts have relegated such ministry to those performing psychotherapy. This verdict was a decided relief to relatively untrained pastors!

There have been notable exceptions to this scenario, with First Baptist Atlanta's being a prime example. Dr. Charles Stanley invited one of our directors to establish a counseling center in 1982, which is yet functioning almost 30 years later. Other churches have used our materials and approach, or a similar model, to a lesser degree; but the basic counseling climate remains the same. Christian academia continues to graduate those who qualify for state licensure—in my opinion, a compromise with the world system.

We know that there are faithful pastors around the country who preach the cross; but most of them would freely state, "I am not a counselor"! Also, it is not infrequent that one message is taught from the pulpit (the Cross for the believer) which is contradicted by another in the counseling room.

With my first international mission trip to the Orient in 1978, it became obvious that

"Let Us Rise Up and Build..." the Church!

developing nations were hungry for a people-helping approach that was spiritual and Scriptural, while the churches in Western Europe and North America were steeped in approaches heavily flavored with psychology. Despite the admonition of Colossians 2:8, Christian psychology is the major player on the scene with its proponents accorded positions of influence in the Christian establishment.

Presently, GFI has done training on all six continents with major training done in Argentina, Brazil, Australia, India, Romania, Ukraine, Germany, Kenya, Canada, South Africa, Korea, and the Philippines.

Resources are available for the coming Reformation. Since our first conference in 1972, we have developed materials for use by the Church in training its members. *Handbook to Happiness* (Tyndale) was first marketed in 1972, with *Ins and Out of Rejection* in 1975. The *Handbook* and one of my books on rejection have now been published in English, Spanish, Russian, and Romanian.

Handbook has now been published in ten languages with the *Wheel and Line*, (a condensation of Chapter 2) now translated in 45, with Mongolian, Somali, and Amharic being the latest. More than a dozen books have been published, along with many supplementary materials for thorough training by churches.

Such materials have been time proven, and God has attested to their validity in our ministry and that of others. As a discipleship counseling Reformation gains momentum in the teaching of sanctification by faith, the materials will continue to be used of God to transform lives.

A body of knowledge is being amassed to supplement the teaching of the Church fathers of the past which can be greatly used in teaching Christ as life—not just as Savior and Lord!

"Let Us Rise Up and Build..." the Church!

FORTY YEARS OF GOD'S FAITHFULNESS

As I survey the years gone by
And recount what God has done,
All glory goes to Him
For countless vict'ries won.
Hurting believers turned to Him
In desperate need of healing;
The Holy Spirit met their need
The Cross from the Word revealing. (Gal. 2:20)

Many had suffered needlessly—
Knowing not Jesus as their life;
Though confident of sins forgiven,
They were doomed to years of strife.
As they came to the end of self, (Rom. 7:24)
God was faithful to meet them there;
...*The garment of praise for the spirit of heaviness* (Isa. 61:3a)
As He lifted them from despair.

He healed the halt and lame while here,
And He is faithful to do so now;
But at the shrine of man's answers, (Col. 2:8)
We must steadfastly refuse to bow.

Repairing the Walls

The Spirit moves with consummate ease
Where much effort has been expended;
When such non-answers have proven futile,
His grace remains extended.

Come unto me...ye that are heavy laden
And I will give you rest; (Matt. 11:28)
He will fulfill His promise still,
If we but put Him to the test!
But we must cease from our own works (Heb. 4:10)
Or, else, we will come to grief;
If we fall short of entering in,
It will be because of unbelief. (Heb. 3:19)

Come to Him without delay;
In Him you will find rest. (Heb. 4:9,10)
Losing your life to save it, (Matt. 16:25)
With His life you'll be blessed.
Faithful is He that calleth you,
Who also will do it; (1 Thess. 5:24)
The passing years will only prove
'Twas He Who called you to it.

Charles R. Solomon

"Let Us Rise Up and Build..." the Church!

CHAPTER 4

SANBALLAT AND TOBIAH!
Representing the *Status Quo*, Active and Passive Resistance

Once it became obvious that Nehemiah and the people were serious about rebuilding the wall, the establishment began to oppose, by ridicule and attempted deception. Sanballat and Tobiah were the 'point men' in such activities.

Tobiah said the construction was so poor that even a fox running on it would break down their stone wall (Neh. 4:3). When ridicule failed, Sanballat invited Nehemiah to leave the wall for a consultation with him (Neh. 6:7).

Similarly, while there has been some active resistance over the years, it has been primarily from those in the psychology/counseling arena where their presuppositions are being brought into question. It boils down to a spiritual/theological discipline versus one that is rooted in psychological theory. Or, stated otherwise, is the Holy Spirit the Therapist; or is it an individual practicing therapy?

When the cross is front and center, the disciple/minister is the agent of the Holy Spirit to lead a seeking believer on his journey to the cross. The problem is diagnosed as the flesh, or 'self', as contrasted with its manifestation in psychological and/or behavioral symptoms. The believer practicing therapy in accord with his/her training is intent upon bringing comfort or resolution to such *symptoms*, while the Holy Spirit would deal with their *source*.

When addressed from this vantage point, it will be seen that the Holy Spirit would deal with the *cause* while therapy is concerned with the *result*, thereby assuring a conflict in ideology. Since the Christian community has attempted an integration of the two disciplines, the Christian therapist is at cross purposes. If he(she) has not come to an illumination of the cross in his(her) own life, it is inescapable that some form of self-enhancement would be employed.

Therefore, such a therapist may be totally committed to do spiritual ministry but is lacking in the vital ingredient of the personal knowledge of the death/resurrection process through which to lead another. The result is unwittingly participating in the strengthening of the flesh for its inevitable conflict with the Spirit (Gal. 5:17).

With such a scenario, varying theological persuasions may be embraced by a therapist who is following a psychological model. And, it is frequent that a seminary is supporting the teaching of Christian psychology where the theological position of the school is not embodied. My plea is that there be a one to one correspondence between what is taught in theology and that practiced in the counseling room. If that were true, I would respect them though I might disagree with their theology.

While there have been a number of critical statements made of our model (in person and in writing), they are usually emanating either from a psychological or theological model where the cross is not central. Therefore, attempting to counter such arguments is futile since the presuppositions are irreconcilable with a deeper-life sanctification approach.

Since that is the case, I will only resort to our scriptural foundation, most succinctly stated in Romans, chapter 6, and not participate in a fruitless debate with those who are on a differing spiritual wavelength. Yet, there is room for discussion or dialogue with those who do similar spiritual counseling with the same presuppositions but may follow a different journey to the cross.

Those whose lives have not been transformed, by the Spirit's revealing their identification with Christ in His death and resurrection, must content themselves with some form of integration of psychology and Scripture. However, this approach produces less than miraculous results. Of course, such an

Sanballat and Tobiah!

amalgamation is much more palatable to the Christian press and more acceptable to the Church at large, where this sanctification message is not embraced.

While we love the brethren in both the Church and therapeutic communities, our purpose is not to debate truth but to present it as God has led us these decades and allow the Holy Spirit to use it as He will.

The results which the Spirit has given speak for themselves with many having been similarly used of God in sharing the message of the cross in person, teaching, and/or from the pulpit. I have been in touch recently with one lady I counseled in 1969 and another in the early 70's who are yet walking with our Lord. We are in touch with a number from the 70's, some of whom regularly support the ministry.

The most consistent, and accurate, criticism over the years is that "it is too simplistic"! My usual reply is, "Amen", and that many would be left out if it required advanced education to understand and appropriate. I am thankful that my Lord agrees that simple is good (Mark 10:15)!

CHAPTER 5

JOINING HANDS WITH OTHERS — PAST AND PRESENT
(Neh. 4:20)

The people joined together under the direction of Nehemiah to accomplish the mammoth task and looked to the God of heaven to prosper them (Neh. 2:20). They joined hands almost literally, while we joined hands, figuratively, with those gone before in the history of the Church.

For those desiring to 'pigeon hole' our approach theologically, it is in the general Keswick camp which hosted such spiritual luminaries as Hudson Taylor, Andrew Murray, Hannah Whitall Smith, F. B. Meyer and many others. In Keswick teaching, the cross is central with the emphasis on coming to know Christ as life. The primary difference is that a conference format is utilized in Keswick, where ours has been usually a one on one application.

In Keswick conferences since 1875, the attendees are primarily ministers and missionaries, whereas ours tend toward those with some degree of psychopathology. In either case, it is the transforming work of the Holy Spirit which is central, with the cross as the focus.

In theological circles, the Keswick approach is compared and contrasted with Calvinism or Reformed theology. Since the application of the cross (Rom. 6:6-14) is not central in the Calvinistic approach to sanctification, the teaching is usually that of progressive sanctification. I do not understand generic sanctification to be attended with miraculous life transformation in the near term. Most in Reformed theology would opt for nouthetic counseling which is based on that tradition.

Having given that general connection, our approach places the 'cookies on a lower shelf'. One of the main difficulties of the Keswick conference is that the one-to-one encounter is frequently not available, such that appropriation of Christ as life is not as effectively or efficiently articulated. The individual time allows the Spirit to home in on the exact difficulty in understanding or application of the truth.

In sum, Christ-centered counseling is essentially personal work with a believer, leading one to the cross of identification (Gal. 2:20). This is parallel to the evangelism process whereby an unbeliever is led to Christ's death *for* us for salvation. As such, it embodies the KISS principle: "Keep It Simple Solomon!"

In keeping with this principle, I have written a book and tract on the Romans Road which has historically been only an evangelistic tool. The emphasis of the book is that *the Romans Road does not terminate in the Wilderness* but proceeds on across the Jordan into Canaan (representing the *life hid with Christ in God* [Col. 3:3]). However, limiting the Romans steps only to salvation sentences most believers for many years, to a lifetime, of wandering the wilderness of defeat and carnality; they are saved from sin but not from themselves!

Thus, on the more complete 'Romans Road', justification and sanctification are taught, simultaneously, with some experiencing the cross at the beginning of the journey as it should be, rather than years later, or never!

In reaching out and increasing the faith of the Church to venture into the ministry of the Spirit's transforming believers, I have written *Discipling the Desperate* and *From Pastors to Pastors: Testimonies of Revitalized Ministries*. The first contains more than 60 case studies of those whose lives were changed through cross-oriented counseling, and the second documents more than 30 pastors whose lives and ministries have been profoundly impacted.

In rebuilding the walls of the Church, it is apparent that a new Reformation is needed to showcase the preaching of the cross or sanctification by faith. In the first Reforma-

Joining Hands with Others

tion, the emphasis was necessarily justification by faith; but there was a near exclusion of the teaching of sanctification. This has now become so ingrained that it will require another Reformation to rectify the omission. The first showed from the Scriptures how to receive new life; now, five centuries later, we need to learn to live it. The Church has been in the wilderness so long that, in the thinking of most, the abnormal has become normal!

The printing press heralded, or made possible, the first Reformation; and the internet could pave the way for the second! Since a small percentage of believers ever seem to understand Christ as life, there must be a resurgence of such teaching in understandable fashion if there is to be renewal or revitalization in the Church at this troubled time in its history.

It is our desire to link up, or join hands, with those who are teaching the same message, since such ministries can enhance and encourage each other. Not all can, or should, do one on one discipleship; but the Body of Christ must erase denominational lines and

"Let Us Rise Up and Build..." the Church!

unite in proclaiming *the riches of the glory of this mystery...which is Christ in you the hope of glory* (Col. 1:27b)!

Joining Hands with Others

THE BLOOD AND THE CROSS

Jesus' Blood was shed for sinners
That sins might be expiated;
Only so are we forgiven,
With our spirits regenerated.
The Reformation made this clear
With teaching on justification,
But the sinner—not just sins—
Is the object in sanctification.

Five centuries of justification by faith
Have focused the Church on doing;
But the Spirit would change our thinking
With the Cross central in His wooing.
Sanctification by faith, the heart cry,
Is the urgent need of the Church;
Limiting teaching to sin's forgiveness,
Society will leave it in the lurch!

The Reformation based on the Blood
Was the needed mid-course correction;
A Reformation based on the Cross
Must change the Church's direction.

"Let Us Rise Up and Build..." the Church!

The Blood deals with what we've done
Which changes our destination;
The Cross deals with what we *are*,
Which changes our inclination.

The Church must be revitalized
If the world is to respect her;
Decades of shallow teaching
Have made her message a blur.
With members searching for answers
And few having a life to share,
Only a new Reformation
Will prepare them burdens to bear. (Gal. 6:2)

C. R. Solomon
July 5, 2010

CHAPTER 6

A NEW REFORMATION

The wall of Jerusalem symbolized the Jews as a called out people of God—a place and a people to which those of the captivity might return; it hemmed them in to Himself and, at the same time, barred others from entrance. However, *the wall of Jerusalem also is broken down and the gates thereof are burned with fire* (Neh. 1:3b). So it was reported to Nehemiah by *certain men of Judah*.

The rebuilding of the wall was, to the Jews, similar to what a reformation would be to Christians today—a return to our birthright. The Church received a great boost by the Reformation in which Luther was prominent. Once again, the Church is in desperate need of renewal.

"Let Us Rise Up and Build..." the Church!

Based on the foregoing accounting of our Lord's ministration of personal revival to those who experience the cross in discipleship or sanctification, it is a foregone conclusion that the Church needs such a visitation. Though many are honestly and earnestly praying for revival, they frequently expect a major outpouring of the Spirit on a congregation or community, as has been the case in previous great awakenings. While I believe such prayer should continue, genuine personal revival can take place as individual believers experience the cross through scriptural teaching of sanctification.

Then, as one believer shares the fullness of the cross with another, personal revival can spread to the Church and community. Major awakenings of the past, such as the Welsh revival of the early 1900's, had life transformations by the Holy Spirit; but those affected were not taught the place the cross had in such transformations. Therefore, the revival began to die out; and the question usually asked is, "How do we maintain revival?" Much study and research have been

A New Reformation

done on this topic which tend to center on revivals which did not continue.

That vital missing ingredient, which we are espousing in this booklet, was added in the excellent writing of Jessie Penn-Lewis and others of that time. However, it was too late to keep the revival fires burning. Though the lives were transformed and the believers were filled with the Spirit, they did not have articulated to them the work of the cross; thus, they did not know to deny themselves and take up the cross daily (Luke 9:23) and experience continued (2 Cor. 4:11) revival as their minds were renewed. That being the case, a New Reformation is desperately needed, based on sanctification by faith which centers on this vital missing dimension (Rom. 6-8).

As the cross becomes revealed reality in believers' lives, the Holy Spirit will take control, bringing personal revival that will gradually spread to the Body of Christ. Thus, the prayer for general revival will be answered by the Holy Spirit, with the work of the cross having equal emphasis with that of the filling of the Spirit.

It is my conviction that the major awakenings were corrective measures, necessitated by the lack of balanced teaching of the cross and the Spirit. This should have been, and should now be, the normal ministry of the Church!

Since the first Reformation was lacking in this regard, the corrective measures of the Spirit should be recognized by the Church so that a New Reformation makes the truth of the cross in sanctification or discipleship common teaching. Though there are pockets of such teaching, the Church must awaken to its responsibility to herald the teaching of sanctification by faith that new born believers, as well as older believers, might know and live out of their birthright.

Though we are indebted to the Reformers for the revival of justification by faith from the first century or New Testament era, we are equally in need of a revival of sanctification by faith in a New Reformation. With such teaching, the resulting revival can be continuous with the transformed believers reaching out to a lost and dying world.

I believe the following poem captures the need for a New Reformation:

THE REFORMATION REVISITED

The tenets of scripture
Are there for all to receive,
But they're only availed
By those who believe.
While the world holds
That we see to believe;
In the spiritual realm,
We believe to receive.

The cry of the Reformation
Was justification by faith,
Contrary to current teaching
Decrying the Spirit's breath.
Denial of mixing faith and works
Earned Luther persecution;
Staunch adherence to faith alone
Brought spiritual revolution.

A renaissance in thinking
Has begun to take place;
Having been saved by faith alone, (Rom. 1:17b)
We've been adding works to grace. (Gal. 3:3)

A New Reformation

Faith alone has been the cry,
While in salvation receiving;
With spiritual growth, too often,
Being the product of achieving.

The Reformation needs be revisited—
Sanctification by faith alone,
With the cry, *O wretched man* (Rom. 7:24)
While on our faces prone.
With Spirit-sent revival,
Our lives, not built, but lost, (Matt. 16:25)
The new life that He gives
Ours free at so great cost!

The Church waits for revival
Oblivious to its taking place,
With the Spirit's pouring life
Into believers through faith by grace.
Revival shared from one to one
Can bring new life to our nation;
As churches catch the vision,
We'll know discipleship reformation!

"Let Us Rise Up and Build..." the Church!

CHAPTER 7

THE PRAISE OF EZRA AND OURS!
(Neh. 8:6)

As Ezra was called to lead praise from the Word when/after the walls were completed, I believe it is appropriate that we close on a note of praise! Christ-centered counseling ministries are seeing the walls of sanctification being erected by the Holy Spirit with great transformation of lives—here and around the world.

Since I began writing this book, we have had such a report of God's working from a sister in Pennsylvania. She telephoned our office for help for her husband and adult son. As I shared the cross with her on the phone, she was ready to 'lose her life' in exchange

"Let Us Rise Up and Build..." the Church!

for that of the Lord Jesus. She had the same problem, self, as did her husband and son—just different symptoms!

Now, two weeks later, she called and left a message of praise and appreciation for the major change in her own life; and both of her men are responding to the message such that they are studying together! The day after I talked to her, a brother came from North Carolina to my home for two hours on Saturday morning and found victory by nightfall!

And just today, I have witnessed a brother from Texas break into victory, with his adult son on the brink. God is still moving in lives, and local churches could see such transformations on a daily basis when the message of the cross in its fullness is faithfully proclaimed from the Word.

Let's close Part I by giving God the glory since His Spirit illuminates His Word to the renewing of minds and transformation of lives (Rom. 12:2)!

The Praise of Ezra and Ours!

GOD'S FAITHFULNESS TO THE END

Lord God, You've been *my trust*
From the days of *my youth*, (Ps. 71:5b)
From the time that You called me (Isa. 58:10,11)
To make simple a blessed truth. (Gal. 2:20)
You are *my strong habitation* (Ps. 71:3a)
To Whom *I may continually resort*; (Ps. 71:3a, John 15:5)
Thou art my rock and my fortress (Ps. 71:3b)
That Your children I may exhort.

My mouth shall speak t*hy righteousness* (Ps. 71:15a)
And thy salvation all the day;
I will go in thy *strength,* (Ps. 71:16a)
Since mine will not hold sway. (Ps. 71:15b)
You have *taught me from my youth*; (Ps. 71:17a)
And I have *thy wondrous works declared,* (Ps. 71:17b)
That Your Church might be set free
From worldly wisdom which has ensnared. (Col. 2:8)

Now that *I am old and grayheaded*, (Ps. 71:18a)
O God, please do not *forsake me*;
Until I have shown thy strength (Ps. 71:18b)
And this generation's guide You make me. (Ps. 71:18b)

"Let Us Rise Up and Build..." the Church!

Thy righteousness, O God, is very high, (Ps. 71:19a)
And You have *done great things;* (Ps. 71:19a)
My soul, which Thou hast redeemed, (Ps. 71:23b)
And all that is within me, sings! (Ps. 71:22, 23)

C. R. Solomon
May 23, 2009

PART II

THE CHURCH WITHOUT
(Matt. 16:18)

"Let Us Rise Up and Build..." the Church!

AN OVERVIEW

Grace Fellowship International (GFI) was called into existence of God in the late 1960's to provide His answer to those in deep distress through the instrumentality of discipleship counseling. Compared to the traditional approaches to counseling, it is revolutionary since it is attended by miracles wrought in the lives by the Holy Spirit. The reformation that is so urgently needed in the field of counseling could well be the means by which God brings revival to the Church. Reform movements are seldom popular with those entrenched in commonly accepted theories and practices. Likewise, reformers are likely to find their greatest acceptance in some place other than their own homes and home towns, or posthumously!

"Let Us Rise Up and Build..." the Church!

Literally thousands of transformed lives around the world attest to God's honoring this specialized counseling approach known as *Spirituotherapy*; and the requests for help and interest in training, in this and other countries, underscore the desperate need to make it available on a worldwide basis. The techniques are proven; materials are available; and a host of men and women called of God stand ready to spearhead an international movement. It has taken a number of years to lay a solid foundation; now it is time to build on the precedent of more than 4 decades of ministry and training.

I am convinced that what we do must be done quickly, or the opportunity will be forever lost. The world situation is not unlike that of Nehemiah when he was burdened and called of the Lord to rebuild the walls of Jerusalem. Let's do a flashback and compare our situation to his:

> *Then said I unto them, ye see the distress we are in, how the wall of Jerusalem lieth waste,*

An Overview

> *and the gates thereof are burned with fire: come, and let us build up the wall of Jerusalem, that we be no more a reproach. Then I told them of the hand of my God which was good upon me; as also the king's words that he had spoken unto me. And they said, Let us rise up and build. So they strengthened their hands for this good work* (Neh. 2:17-20).

As with Nehemiah of old, I would ask you soberly to consider the ominous clouds on the horizon and "see the distress that we are in" (Neh. 2:17):

1. *See the distress we are in as individuals* — One has only to sit in the counseling room for a short period of time to be apprized of the heartache and heartbreak which abound in epidemic proportions in the lives of Christians! If believers are falling apart due to the shallowness

of their faith, what chance does an unbeliever have in a world which is rapidly becoming chaotic? Only the believer who is firmly anchored in his resources in Christ will be able to stand as adverse conditions become the rule, rather than the exception! Sunday Christians who are already falling by the wayside, will be of little or no value in the heat of the battle. Disciples are formed in the crucible of suffering, and many Christians are presently enrolled in crash courses!

2. *See the distress we are in as families* — The average Christian family is no longer a model which can be held up as an example of love and solidarity to an unbelieving world. Christian marriages, or rather marriages in which the partners happen to be Christians, are being torn asunder with divorce becoming commonplace. Many of these remarry without serious consideration of their scriptural position. The children of broken marriages are emotionally dam-

An Overview

aged by parents who choose to escape a bad set of circumstances rather than stay and let God transform their lives and marriage. The emotional damage, and lack of spiritual training enjoined upon the parents by the scriptures, couple together to program the child of such a union to do a repeat performance in his own marriage.

3. *See the distress we are in as a local church* — The typical local church is ill-equipped to meet the desperate needs in the individuals and families. Many are doing yeoman's service in the ministry of evangelism but are woefully inadequate in the arena of discipleship. The Lord Jesus Christ made discipleship an option; most Christians and, therefore, most churches have opted out! Pastors have not, and do not, receive adequate clinical discipleship training to deal with pathological conditions within, and between, individuals. This being the case, the same pathology spills

over into the local church. Christianity, in the main, has become superficial; and so have relationships between the members of most churches. Probably most of the members are suffering from alienation and are desperately seeking love, acceptance and meaningful relationships. Absent this, many are turning to worldly pursuits, or even to cults, to fill the ever present vacuum. The walls of the Church are down, and its members are straying to anything which betokens some relief from the pain of emptiness; empty people are vainly trying to fill each other! God ordained the Church to reach people for Christ and to minister to their needs. Only as the Church is strong in the Lord can it become God's instrument to stem the tide of impending anarchy and chaos.

4. *See the distress we are in as a Nation*—We can no longer consider our nation to be Christian. The breakdown of the fam-

ily, and the mediocre brand of Christianity which obtains today, leave the nation with little in the way of spiritual backbone. Economic inflation and energy shortages are combining to short-circuit materialism which has become a way of life to a myriad of persons. The deflation of the spiritual resources causes selfishness to be rampant, resulting in citizens fighting each other rather than pulling together when faced with adverse circumstances such as fuel shortages or unemployment. The cancer of sin and secularism which is eating away at the innards of our country makes it vulnerable to internal and external forces. The spiritual debilitation experienced by the nation has rendered us all but impotent to remain a major force for good, and for God, in the world today.

5. *See the distress we are in as a world*—From the Middle East to the Far East there is more turmoil, disaster, and shortages of

food and energy than in any previous 'peace time' era in history. The energy crisis has whole nations on the brink of bankruptcy, which all but has them at the mercy of the oil producing nations. As the scarcity of energy and goods looms larger and larger, nation will be at the throat of nation to garner as much as possible for themselves. Lacking mutual cooperation, the parts will destroy the whole except as ordained by God and His direct intervention.

THE WALLS ARE DOWN

1. *The walls of commitment:* Thorough-going commitment to anything other than the pursuit of possessions, pleasure, and power is largely a thing of the past. Total commitment to God's purpose for our lives is unselfish, and self-abnegation has never been popular! It takes more commitment to join some lodges

or country clubs than it does many churches.

2. *The walls of separation from worldly methods:* More humanism has infiltrated the Church than we care to admit. Its effect is probably more pronounced in counseling, in that much Christian counseling is merely scripture wrapped around a humanistic core. Some who faithfully practice separation from the world in matters concerning sin, rely upon the arm of the flesh by using methodology and counseling approaches developed by the world system. Many devoted Christians who are utilizing such approaches are not aware of the deleterious effects of adding scripture to psychology, rather than adding psychology to scripture where there is no conflict.

3. *The walls of discipleship:* True discipleship involves the experienced cross. Luke 14:27 states:

> *And whosoever doth not bear his cross and come after me, cannot be my disciple".*

This truth is foreign to the majority of believers, which is the cause of near impotence on the part of the local church to minister effectively to disturbed persons. Either we will be *crucified to the world* (Gal 6:14). or we will succumb to it! We are most unlikely to make an impact on the world for Christ, if we are yet controlled by the world.

The Hand of My God is Upon Me

As God revealed the answer to my needs through coming to know Christ as Life (Gal. 2:20), He began to burden me to share with other hurting individuals. This is the *King's word that he spoke unto me*:

> *And if thou draw out thy soul to the hungry; and satisfy the*

An Overview

> *afflicted soul; then shall thy light rise in obscurity, and thy darkness be as the noon day; and the Lord shall guide thee continually, and satisfy thy soul in drought, and make fat thy bones; and thou shalt be like a watered garden, and like a spring of water, whose waters fail not* (Isa. 58:10, 11).

> *Behold, I have refined thee, but not with silver; I have chosen thee in the furnace of affliction. For mine own sake, even mine own sake, will I do it; for how should my name be polluted: and I will not give my glory to another* (Isa. 48:10,11).

God had given a vision and a call for the establishment of a Christ-centered counseling approach on a world-wide basis. Very few shared this vision at the beginning, and many were vocal in their opposition.

> *Then answered I them, and said unto them, The God of heaven, he will prosper us; therefore we his servants will arise and build* (Neh. 2:20a).

God, indeed, has prospered us and has transformed thousands of lives to the place that they, in turn, have been His instruments of ministry to others. Many of you have already joined hands with us as His servants and have been used in laying the foundation upon which the walls are to be built.

In addition to the vision and the call, He also gave a promise:

> *And they that shall be of thee shall build up the old waste places: thou shalt raise up the foundations of many generations; and thou shalt be called, The repairer of the breach, The restorer of paths to dwell in Isa. 58:12.*

An Overview

Now, I lay a challenge before you to take before God in prayer: Neh. 1:20b is addressed to those who opposed Nehemiah:

> . . . *but ye have no portion, nor right, nor memorial in Jerusalem.*

Since you belong to the Lord, you do have a right; will you have a portion—in prayer, in ministry, financially, or in whatever way God would lead you to become involved—that you might have a *memorial*!?

"Let Us Rise Up and Build..." the Church!

NO OTHER FOUNDATION

The foundation has been laid
Which is Jesus Christ our Lord, (1 Cor. 3:11)
To build a spiritual house (1 Pet. 2:5)
In accordance with His Word. (1 Pet. 2:6)
Unto believers He is precious, (1 Pet. 2:7)
Being those who are lively stones— (1 Pet. 2:5)
A priesthood offering sacrifices (1 Pet. 2:5, Rom.12:1)
For whose sin He atones.

Each stone is custom fitted
To fulfill its unique niche;
Resisting the Builder's prep work
Can cause us to be a glitch.
Each of us has a role to fill;
Some need chiseling, others sanded.
But key stones require more work—
Needing breaking to be quite candid!

The Builder knows the schedule
He is never early, never late;
The preparation of each stone
Is timed to the Master's rate.
When the spiritual house is finished,
Spiritual sacrifices can be made;
They're acceptable to God by Jesus Christ
Since the Chief corner stone is laid. (1 Pet. 2:6)

An Overview

The Church is a spiritual house
God's purposes to make known;
For all to be fully realized,
He will need each 'lively stone'. (1 Pet. 2:5)
Each life is to glorify Him
As one and all take their place,
Submitting to the preparation
Which is through faith by grace.

He is ready to transform lives
Of those who take up the Cross; (Luke 9:23,24)
Unwillingness to lose their lives
Will be but to suffer loss.
Then the eyes of the watching world
Will see what God has done,
And all glory will go to Him
For the many victories won.

Charles R. Solomon

"Let Us Rise Up and Build..." the Church!

EPILOGUE

Part 1
Broken to be Filled

As we survey the current Church scene, the most pressing need is that of discipleship. And yet, this is the least emphasized ministry of the typical church.

For the Church to have this vision, and effectively to implement it from the top down, it means that the top leadership must be disciples if they are to model discipleship by precept and example.

It is a foregone conclusion that the pastor should be a disciple. In most Baptist churches the deacons (and/or elders) have a prominent role in leadership. Most quote Acts 6:3 to affirm the requirements that, for a man to qualify for the role of deacon, he must be *...full of the Holy Ghost and wisdom*.

If that is to be the litmus test, how would this be determined; and who will make such a determination? The hackneyed adage is that it takes one to know one! It seems to me that to be filled with the Spirit and to be a disciple are different ways of saying the same thing. In order to be filled with the Spirit, one must be emptied of self; and to be a disciple, one must take up the cross (Luke 14:27). To be filled with self and the Spirit, simultaneously, would be a contradiction!

And, yet, the list of requirements for becoming a deacon does not typically require a testimony and track record of having experienced the cross. To go a step farther, my conversation and experience in counseling with pastors over the last four decades has been that the majority of pastors who have experienced the Cross of identification with Christ are in the ministry several, to many, years before brokenness and filling with the Spirit become a revealed reality. In the excellent biography, *Hudson Taylor's Spiritual Secret*, we find that he was on the mission field between 10 and 15 years before this became a reality in his own life (see *Pastors to Pastors, Testimonies of Revitalized Ministries* by the author).

Epilogue

I personally counseled with one Baptist pastor who had been saved 48 years before the filling of the Spirit or discipleship became a reality for him. Obviously, he could not make disciples if he were not one! At age 69 and retired from ministry, he learned the victorious half of the gospel and left behind no disciples from his personal ministry which is a travesty on the gospel!

I am afraid this is repeated in Baptist churches (and others) more frequently than we would care to admit. Dynamic discipleship would render most counseling unnecessary, since transformed lives result from cross-oriented scriptural discipleship.

However, few pastors personally disciple their staff; and, usually, the staff does not disciple the leaders reporting to them with the full message of the Cross. But it stands to reason that the rank and file Christian will not be making full disciples of those with whom they share the gospel.

This being the case, the preaching of the cross for the believer (Rom. 6:6, Gal. 2:20) is not front and center in the vast majority of churches. This has rendered the Church all but impotent and has resulted in a movement of 'seeker sensitive' churches with most *having a form of godliness, but denying the power thereof* (2 Tim. 3:15).

As the unemployment and underemployment situation continues to worsen, the Church will be called upon to minister, not only to material needs, but also to rampant spiritual needs and deficiencies. But, from top to bottom, the Church itself is in urgent need of equipping so that both pastor and people are adequately readied for such ministry.

It has been my experience, in the churches I have attended, that there is no requirement that deacons give testimony of having experienced the cross (are filled with the Spirit) and have learned to walk in the Spirit and articulate it to others. It is obvious that the pastor must set the pace in both instances, if he is to teach by example as well as precept.

From 40 years of discipleship ministry, with not a little to pastors and missionaries,

Epilogue

I think it is safe to say that a small percentage of members have experienced the cross of identification; and of those who have, few are able to lead another into such victory or the Spirit-filled life.

It seems that churches could well define the end result that they believe is scriptural for believers and then design a ministry that produces that desired result. However, it seems that many, if not most, are on a maintenance regimen, with little vision or determination to forsake the 'arm of the flesh' in ministry. We have had decades of ministering in human strength such the abnormal has become normal; so much so, that a Spirit-filled believer may almost be a rarity in the typical church.

A return to preaching the cross and dynamic sanctification is an absolute necessity if the Church is to approximate the New Testament quality of disciple-making in its role and destiny. It will probably require a new Reformation with the cry of 'sanctification by faith' if Christ's cross is to be central in life and ministry. Anything short of this will

"Let Us Rise Up and Build..." the Church!

result in the Church's being neutralized, or marginalized, by secularism to the detriment of the Kingdom!

Epilogue

Part 2
The Task of the Church Today

Recent decades have seen a decrease in the impact of the Church on the culture. Since it has been a time of relative ease from the standpoint of economics and social acceptability, it has tended to let down its guard and has tended to drift downward into mediocrity.

While it has prospered in faces, finances and facilities, the spiritual growth has been inversely proportional due to de-emphasizing discipleship. Much of the discipleship which takes place tends to be teaching the disciplines of the Christian life rather than the life in Christ. Luke 14:27 gives us the *sine qua non* of discipleship which is taking up our cross or losing our lives in order to save them (Luke 9:24).

However, most Christians are still living their independent lives, even living for the Lord, and are frequently taught that they

"Let Us Rise Up and Build..." the Church!

can do that while being a 'learner'; a caricature of true discipleship. Galatians 2:20 and Romans 6 must become front and center in the teaching of the Church, if it is to be empowered to face the multiple challenges immediately ahead.

Since the economic situation will, in all likelihood, continue to spiral downward, it will be faced with members in dire need at a time when its income will also be curtailed. Therefore, it behooves the Church to make spiritual preparations for ministry in adverse circumstances (circumstances that include a negative governmental role).

Not only will it need strength to minister internally, the Church must also be empowered to confront the establishment from a standpoint of spiritual strength arising from the cross. This is, however, not the stance of the typical evangelical church. Nor has such a Church been friendly in recent decades to the message of the cross in sanctification.

Added to this mix is the fact that Islam has declared a Holy War (which, by definition, is a spiritual war). That being the case,

Epilogue

it is incumbent upon the Church to prepare for its role in such a conflict. However, it has been my experience that churches are not taking seriously their responsibility, but tend toward 'business as usual', despite the fact that it is anything but usual!

When Islam is constantly proving that it is ready to fight *to* the death in a spiritual conflict, it is rather obvious that the Church must be ready to fight *from* the death (Col. 3:3) if it is to have power to be triumphant so that the gates of Hell do not prevail against it. Only as the Cross is our rallying cry will the Church be empowered to raise the banner of *Thus saith the Lord*.

Attempts to confront Islam in the strength of the flesh will be futile; absent the experienced cross, that is precisely what it will be doing. Preparation for a Holy War must be a concerted effort, with all necessary materials and training exercises, proven over 39 years, presently available. However, the Church must avail herself of that which is needful.

"Let Us Rise Up and Build..." the Church!

The serious believer must truly become a Soldier of the Cross (see the following poem). Such training is documented in my book, *Handbook for Soldiers of the Cross*; and basic training could be done by a church in as little as ten (10) days. However, as we found in World War II, it is a little late to train and equip an army after the war has been declared!

But, I believe most are oblivious to the war presently in progress since it is a spiritual war, and yet some churches espouse interfaith collaboration. How can two walk together except they be agreed?

In summary, we must reassess the milieu in which we are ministering and put on the whole armor of God, or we will be soundly defeated in a very real spiritual battle. Sunday morning Christianity, and catering to the wants and desires of 'seekers', will only prepare us for disaster! Only churches filled with disciples will be a formidable deterrent to the forces of darkness which are arrayed against them.

Epilogue

More than four decades have passed since God called me to such ministry in 1967, and He has honored His calling with transformed lives on six continents. Churches, likewise, can see lives transformed daily if the preaching of the cross (1 Cor. 1:18) is the vital and consistent message; then, they can be equipped to be *ambassadors for Christ* (2 Cor. 5:20a).

The Church of the twenty-first century must have a correspondence to the Church of the first century if it is to speak faith, hope, and love to an alien culture in conflict.

"Let Us Rise Up and Build..." the Church!

SOLDIERS OF THE CROSS

Are you a soldier of the Cross,
Marching to our Lord's command;
Do you even know there is a war
Raging throughout the land?
The inroads of the Enemy
Are causing widespread destruction;
Many of us are lulled to sleep,
Since his strategy is seduction.

The loss of life and casualties
Stagger the imagination—
Multiplied millions of babies killed,
With the approval of our nation.
Millions of others have been seduced
By cults, New Age, and gay pride;
Many of these have never heard—
There is freedom in the Crucified. (John 8:32,36)

The good news of the Gospel
Has been taught without its power; (2 Tim. 3:5)
Absent the victory of the Cross,
Soldiers tend to retreat and cower.

Epilogue

We meet in enclaves to worship
And depart to do our thing;
And Enemy forces unite to fight,
While we our choruses sing!

Political candidates garner votes,
Sanctioning abortion and perversion—
The faith of our fathers undermined
By ill-disguised forms of subversion.
Mandates of God's Word forsaken
In favor of gay rights and pro-choice;
Opponents of the right are exalted—
The truth all but denied a voice.

All that's required for evil to win
Is for believers to do nothing;
The Cross of Christ, the power of God, (1 Cor. 1:18)
Replaced by lies in New Age clothing.
Churches go about business as usual,
Answering questions people aren't asking;
The Enemy's plan pushes full-bore ahead,
With believers, in salvation basking.

Soldiers in God's tattered army
Are ill-fed, ill-trained, and defeated;
Unless we awake and don our armor, (Eph. 6:10,11)
Sodom and Gomorrah will be repeated.

"Let Us Rise Up and Build..." the Church!

God is looking for righteous men
Who are willing to stand in the gap; (Ez. 22:30)
Suffering and sacrifice are the watchwords—
Victory will not just fall in our lap!

Self-serving—not self-sacrifice—
Has been the order of the day;
A generation has been spawned
That has rarely heard The Way.
Peace, peace, when there is no peace, (Jer. 6:14b)
Is the Enemy's battle cry;
Those accustomed to the 'good life'
Are conditioned to believe the lie.

Our freedoms are rapidly eroding;
We have taken our blessings for granted.
Will God grant us a reprieve,
While His Word and Life are implanted?
It is no longer a matter of choice;
It will soon be a fight for survival.
Human effort will no longer avail;
Our only hope is Holy Spirit revival.

Are you ready for revival to come
And to have it begin in you?
Are you ready your life to lose,
That yours He might live through?

Epilogue

The Cross is no longer optional;
And, really, it never has been.
Our life to save we must lose, (Matt. 16:25)
If we are a new life to begin.

Preaching the Cross, the power of God, (1 Cor. 1:18)
Is the message believers need;
But the pleasure-mad throng drives onward—
Blinded by self, and refusing to heed.
It is not easy ourselves to deny (Luke 9:23,24)
And to find our meaning in Him; (Col. 3:4)
But without revival in the Church,
The future of our nation is dim.

His challenge to us is simple:
Allow the Spirit our hearts to search; (Ps. 139:23,24)
Only as we're transformed, one by one, (Rom. 12:2)
Will there be life in His Body, the Church.
The world has chosen darkness; (John 3:19)
Humanism and sin are a blight.
We must die in order to live,
If to the world we're to be the light. (Matt. 5:14,16)

I am dead with Christ yet I live, (Gal. 2:20)
And as the branch in the vine, I abide; (John 15:5)
The world is crucified unto me;
Unto the world I am crucified. (Gal. 6:14)

"Let Us Rise Up and Build..." the Church!

All is not lost, if we're willing to lose
Our lives as the Scripture saith; (John 12:25)
Thanks be to God for triumph in Christ (2 Cor. 2:14)
As we overcome the world by faith. (1 John 5:4)

>Charles R. Solomon
>1991

RESOURCES AVAILABLE FROM GRACE FELLOWSHIP INTERNATIONAL

Books by Dr. Charles Solomon:

Handbook to Happiness
Ins and Out of Rejection
Rejection Syndrome and the Way to Acceptance
Handbook to Happiness & You
Handbook for Christ-Centered Counseling
Handbook for Soldiers of the Cross
Handbook to Happiness for the Church
For Me To Live Is Christ
The Romans Road
From Pastors to Pastors — Testimonies of Revitalized Ministries
Discipling the Desperate — The Spirit's Ministry to Hurting Believers
The Wisdom of (Charles R.) Solomon 2 Volume Poetry Set
Gems & Jargon
Wheel & Line Tract
Romans Road Tract

"Let Us Rise Up and Build…" the Church!

Books by Dr. John Woodward:

Blessed Reassurance
Man as Spirit, Soul, and Body
Weekly e-devotional GraceNotes

Media Materials:

Conference Audio CDs
Conference DVDs
Conference Notebook

Book by Dr. Phil Jones:

How To Exchange Your Life For A New One

Books by Dr. Lee Turner:

Grace Discipleship Course #1
Grace Discipleship Course #2

Book by Captain Reginald Wallis:

The New Life

CPSIA information can be obtained at www.ICGtesting.com
Printed in the USA
LVOW091142280112

266005LV00001B/1/P